The Big Jazz Band

by Diego Vargas

illustrated by Hector Borlasca

Target Skill Consonants Vv/v/, Zz/z/
High-Frequency Words *where, come*

Scott Foresman
is an imprint of

Jan and Dad zip up.

Jan and Dad get in the van.

They see Jem and Dad.
"Can you come with us?
You will like it."

Jem and Dad get in the van.
Jan is glad Jem can come.

Dad sees Bev.

Dad stops the van next to a bus.

"Come with me," said Bev.
"You will like it.
You will see a big jazz band."

The jazz band is big.
Jan and Jem have fun.
Do you like it?

Where did you go?

We went to see a big jazz band.

It was fun.